Walt Disney

by Joanne Mattern

Content Consultant

Nanci R. Vargus, Ed.D.
Professor Emeritus, University of Indianapolis

Reading Consultant

Jeanne Clidas, Ph.D.

Children's Press®
An Imprint of Scholastic Inc.
New York Toronto London Auckland Sydney
Mexico City New Delhi Hong Kong
Danbury, Connecticut

Cataloging-in-Publication Data is available from the Library of Congress

ISBN 978-0-531-24740-2 (lib. bdg.)
ISBN 978-0-531-24706-8 (pbk.)

Produced by Spooky Cheetah Press
Poem by Jodie Shepherd

Printed in China 62

SCHOLASTIC, CHILDREN'S PRESS, ROOKIE BIOGRAPHIES®, and associated logos are trademarks and/or registered trademarks of Scholastic Inc.

1 2 3 4 5 6 7 8 9 10 R 22 21 20 19 18 17 16 15 14 13

Photographs © 2013: Alamy Images: 3 bottom (AF archive), 3 top left (Greg Balfour Evans), 12 (Pictorial Press Ltd.); AP Images/PRNewsFoto/Disneyland, Scott Brinegar: 28, 31 bottom; Corbis Images/Bettmann: 15; Dreamstime: 31 center bottom (Radu Razvan Gheorghe), 24 (Silvestrovairina), 27, 30 right (Wangkun Jia); Everett Collection: 20 bottom (Walt Disney), 19, 20 top; Getty Images: cover, 4, 11, 31 center top (Hulton Archive); Library of Congress: 8; Superstock, Inc./imagebroker.net: 3 top right; The Image Works/TopFoto: 16, 31 top; The Picture Desk/Walt Disney Pictures/The Kobal Collection: 23.

Maps by XNR Productions, Inc.

Table of Contents

Meet Walt Disney

Walt Disney was a famous **artist**. He was the creator of Mickey Mouse. Walt drew many cartoons and made movies. He also created the **theme parks** Disneyland and Walt Disney World.

This photo shows Walt drawing a scene from *Steamboat Willie*.

Walt was born on December 5, 1901, in Chicago, Illinois. He had three brothers and one sister.

Walt was born in Illinois.

MAP KEY

▨ Illinois

● City where
  Walt Disney
  was born

Wisconsin

Michigan

Lake
Michigan

Iowa

Chicago ●

Illinois

Indiana

Missouri

Kentucky

Arkansas

Tennessee

As a boy, Walt wrote plays with his friends. They put on shows onstage. But more than anything, Walt loved to draw. He drew funny cartoons for his friends.

FAST FACT!

Walt worked hard, too. He got up at 3:30 in the morning to deliver newspapers. Then he went to school.

Walt took night classes at an art school while he was in high school. The United States was at war at the time. Walt wanted to help. So he left school to drive an ambulance in the war.

Walt drove an ambulance like this one. He added drawings to the sides of his ambulance.

After the war, Walt went back to his favorite activity: drawing cartoons. He and his brother Roy started their own **animation studio**. Walt invented characters like Mickey Mouse, Minnie Mouse, and Donald Duck.

Roy and Walt at work at Disney Brothers Studio

Walt met his wife, Lillian, at the Disney Brothers Studio. She worked there. Walt and Lillian fell in love and were married in 1925. They later had two daughters, Diane and Sharon.

This picture of Walt's family was taken when Diane was 16 and Sharon was 13.

Mickey Mouse and Friends

In 1928, Walt made a short movie called *Steamboat Willie*. The star was Mickey Mouse. *Steamboat Willie* was the first cartoon to put sound with pictures. It was a hit!

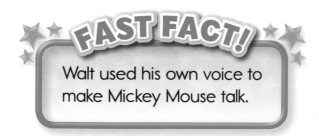

FAST FACT!

Walt used his own voice to make Mickey Mouse talk.

In 1937, Walt made his first full-length movie. It was called *Snow White and the Seven Dwarfs*. Many people saw the film. Then Walt made more popular movies: *Pinocchio*, *Fantasia*, and *Bambi*.

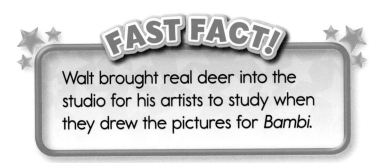

FAST FACT!

Walt brought real deer into the studio for his artists to study when they drew the pictures for *Bambi*.

The movie poster for *Snow White and the Seven Dwarfs*

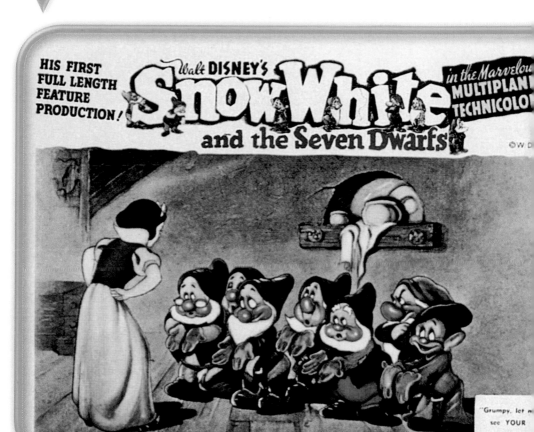

TV Time

Walt also created television shows. Every week, families gathered in front of the TV to watch. Walt's first program showed Disney movies.

Walt's first television series was on TV for a long time. First it was shown in black and white and then in color.

Another show Walt created was *The Mickey Mouse Club*. This show was on every day and starred a group of kids known as "Mouseketeers."

FAST FACT!

The Mickey Mouse Club was on TV for many years and starred different Mouseketeers. Britney Spears, Justin Timberlake, and Christina Aguilera were all Mouseketeers when they were young.

23

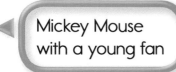

Mickey Mouse
with a young fan

A Happy Place

Walt wanted to build a place where families could have fun. In 1955, he opened a theme park called Disneyland in California. Walt called it "the happiest place on Earth."

FAST FACT!

Walt said Disneyland would never be finished. He was always adding something new to the park.

Walt planned another theme park, in Florida. It was called Walt Disney World. Walt also kept on making movies. Mickey Mouse and his cartoon friends were famous all over the world.

Fireworks light up the sky over Cinderella Castle in Walt Disney World.

27

Timeline of Walt Disney's Life

1923
starts his own movie studio

1928
releases *Steamboat Willie*

1901
born on December 5

Mickey and friends enjoy a ride at Disneyland.

Walt died on December 15, 1966. But he lives on through the characters and parks that he created. His work continues to make people happy.

1937
releases *Snow White and the Seven Dwarfs*

1966
dies on December 15

1955
Disneyland opens in California

1971
Walt Disney World opens in Florida

A Poem About Walt Disney

From Mickey Mouse to Disneyland—
Each one Walt thought up, drew, and planned;
and each fantastic, fun creation
began in Walt's imagination.

You Can Be an Artist

- Practice drawing every day to get good at it.

- Draw pictures of your family and friends. Draw pictures of things you imagine.

Glossary

animation (AN-i-may-shun): cartoon drawings shown very quickly one after another on a screen so that it appears as if the drawings are moving

artist (AR-tist): someone very skilled at painting, making things, or performing

studio (STOO-dee-oh): a place where movies are made or where artists work

theme parks (THEME PARKS): places with rides, games, and other activities

Index

Facts for Now

Visit this Scholastic Web site for more information on Walt Disney:
www.factsfornow.scholastic.com
Enter the keywords **Walt Disney**

About the Author

Joanne Mattern has written more than 250 books for children. She especially likes writing biographies because she loves to learn about real people and the things they do. Joanne also enjoys writing about science, nature, and history. She grew up in New York State and still lives there with her husband, her four children, and an assortment of pets.